A Reflective Self-Care Journal for
Foster and Adoptive Parents

Time
Out

LeShawnda Fitzgerald

TIME -OUT
A REFLECTIVE SELF -CARE JOURNAL FOR
FOSTER & ADOPTIVE PARENTS

FOR SPEAKING ENGAGEMENTS VISIT
LESHAWNDAFITZGERALD .COM

WHO SAYS TIME-OUTS ARE JUST FOR KIDS?

TIME OUT: A REFLECTIVE SELF-CARE JOURNAL FOR FOSTER & ADOPTIVE PARENTS

As a foster and adoptive parent myself, I created this journal to encourage fellow foster and adoptive parents to take time-outs each day for self-care. Regular time-outs can help us manage our stress and emotions, creating opportunities to regulate, realign, reconnect with ourselves and gain valuable perspective and appreciation.

I know firsthand being a foster and adoptive parent can be both a challenging and rewarding experience. Prioritizing our own self-care is necessary in order to provide the best possible care for our children. A daily self-care practice allows us to recharge, refresh and be more resilient to face the challenges of our daily lives. Without self-care we can become overwhelmed, stressed and burnt out, which can negatively impact our own well-being and our ability to parent effectively.

Self-care can also have a positive impact on our children. Children who have experienced trauma or disruption in their lives often benefit from a stable and consistent environment. When parents take care of themselves, they are better able to provide that stability and consistency, which can in turn help children to feel more secure and safe.

Self-care does not have to be time-consuming or expensive. It can be as simple as taking a few minutes each day to practice deep breathing, enjoying a warm cup of tea or completing one of the reflective prompts from this journal.

I hope this journal inspires you to pour into yourself so that you can provide the love and support that your children need from your overflow.

Time-out provides more than 100 affirmations for foster and adoptive parents, along with prompts for journaling and reflection. Take a "time-out" as needed to complete them.

LeShawnda Fitzgerald

LESHAWNDA FITZGERALD
CEO of LeShawndaFitzgerald.com

I am kind to myself.

TODAY I AM FEELING...

_____

_____

_____

I AM TAKING CARE OF MYSELF TODAY BY...

_____

_____

_____

TODAY I AM LOOKING FORWARD TO...

_____

_____

_____

SOMETHING GOOD THAT HAPPENED TODAY...

_____

_____

_____

This moment is a gift.

TODAY I AM FEELING...

_____

_____

_____

I AM TAKING CARE OF MYSELF TODAY BY...

_____

_____

_____

TODAY I AM LOOKING FORWARD TO...

_____

_____

_____

SOMETHING GOOD THAT HAPPENED TODAY...

_____

_____

_____

I feel good.

TODAY I AM FEELING...

_____

_____

_____

I AM TAKING CARE OF MYSELF TODAY BY...

_____

_____

_____

TODAY I AM LOOKING FORWARD TO...

_____

_____

_____

SOMETHING GOOD THAT HAPPENED TODAY...

_____

_____

_____

I am making a difference.

TODAY I AM FEELING...

_____

_____

_____

I AM TAKING CARE OF MYSELF TODAY BY...

_____

_____

_____

TODAY I AM LOOKING FORWARD TO...

_____

_____

_____

SOMETHING GOOD THAT HAPPENED TODAY...

_____

_____

_____

My home is a safe haven.

TODAY I AM FEELING...

_____

_____

_____

I AM TAKING CARE OF MYSELF TODAY BY...

_____

_____

_____

TODAY I AM LOOKING FORWARD TO...

_____

_____

_____

SOMETHING GOOD THAT HAPPENED TODAY...

_____

_____

_____

I can do hard things.

TODAY I AM FEELING...

_____

_____

_____

I AM TAKING CARE OF MYSELF TODAY BY...

_____

_____

_____

TODAY I AM LOOKING FORWARD TO...

_____

_____

_____

SOMETHING GOOD THAT HAPPENED TODAY...

_____

_____

_____

I am loved.

TODAY I AM FEELING...

_____

_____

_____

I AM TAKING CARE OF MYSELF TODAY BY...

_____

_____

_____

TODAY I AM LOOKING FORWARD TO...

_____

_____

_____

SOMETHING GOOD THAT HAPPENED TODAY...

_____

_____

_____

I am supported.

TODAY I AM FEELING...

_____

_____

_____

I AM TAKING CARE OF MYSELF TODAY BY...

_____

_____

_____

TODAY I AM LOOKING FORWARD TO...

_____

_____

_____

SOMETHING GOOD THAT HAPPENED TODAY...

_____

_____

_____

I am doing the best I can.

TODAY I AM FEELING...

_____

_____

_____

I AM TAKING CARE OF MYSELF TODAY BY...

_____

_____

_____

TODAY I AM LOOKING FORWARD TO...

_____

_____

_____

SOMETHING GOOD THAT HAPPENED TODAY...

_____

_____

_____

I am here for a very important reason.

TODAY I AM FEELING...

_____

_____

_____

I AM TAKING CARE OF MYSELF TODAY BY...

_____

_____

_____

TODAY I AM LOOKING FORWARD TO...

_____

_____

_____

SOMETHING GOOD THAT HAPPENED TODAY...

_____

_____

_____

I deserve the best.

TODAY I AM FEELING...

_____

_____

_____

I AM TAKING CARE OF MYSELF TODAY BY...

_____

_____

_____

TODAY I AM LOOKING FORWARD TO...

_____

_____

_____

SOMETHING GOOD THAT HAPPENED TODAY...

_____

_____

_____

I matter.

TODAY I AM FEELING...

_____

_____

_____

I AM TAKING CARE OF MYSELF TODAY BY...

_____

_____

_____

TODAY I AM LOOKING FORWARD TO...

_____

_____

_____

SOMETHING GOOD THAT HAPPENED TODAY...

_____

_____

_____

I am beautiful.

TODAY I AM FEELING...

_____

_____

_____

I AM TAKING CARE OF MYSELF TODAY BY...

_____

_____

_____

TODAY I AM LOOKING FORWARD TO...

_____

_____

_____

SOMETHING GOOD THAT HAPPENED TODAY...

_____

_____

_____

It gets better.

TODAY I AM FEELING...

_____

_____

_____

I AM TAKING CARE OF MYSELF TODAY BY...

_____

_____

_____

TODAY I AM LOOKING FORWARD TO...

_____

_____

_____

SOMETHING GOOD THAT HAPPENED TODAY...

_____

_____

_____

I am strong.

TODAY I AM FEELING...

_____

_____

_____

I AM TAKING CARE OF MYSELF TODAY BY...

_____

_____

_____

TODAY I AM LOOKING FORWARD TO...

_____

_____

_____

SOMETHING GOOD THAT HAPPENED TODAY...

_____

_____

_____

I am safe.

TODAY I AM FEELING...

_____

_____

_____

I AM TAKING CARE OF MYSELF TODAY BY...

_____

_____

_____

TODAY I AM LOOKING FORWARD TO...

_____

_____

_____

SOMETHING GOOD THAT HAPPENED TODAY...

_____

_____

_____

I make healthy choices.

TODAY I AM FEELING...

_____

_____

_____

I AM TAKING CARE OF MYSELF TODAY BY...

_____

_____

_____

TODAY I AM LOOKING FORWARD TO...

_____

_____

_____

SOMETHING GOOD THAT HAPPENED TODAY...

_____

_____

_____

I trust myself.

TODAY I AM FEELING...

_____

_____

_____

I AM TAKING CARE OF MYSELF TODAY BY...

_____

_____

_____

TODAY I AM LOOKING FORWARD TO...

_____

_____

_____

SOMETHING GOOD THAT HAPPENED TODAY...

_____

_____

_____

I am successful.

TODAY I AM FEELING...

_____

_____

_____

I AM TAKING CARE OF MYSELF TODAY BY...

_____

_____

_____

TODAY I AM LOOKING FORWARD TO...

_____

_____

_____

SOMETHING GOOD THAT HAPPENED TODAY...

_____

_____

_____

I am always treated well.

TODAY I AM FEELING...

_____

_____

_____

I AM TAKING CARE OF MYSELF TODAY BY...

_____

_____

_____

TODAY I AM LOOKING FORWARD TO...

_____

_____

_____

SOMETHING GOOD THAT HAPPENED TODAY...

_____

_____

_____

I am surrounded by joy.

TODAY I AM FEELING...

_____

_____

_____

I AM TAKING CARE OF MYSELF TODAY BY...

_____

_____

_____

TODAY I AM LOOKING FORWARD TO...

_____

_____

_____

SOMETHING GOOD THAT HAPPENED TODAY...

_____

_____

_____

Life loves me.

TODAY I AM FEELING...

_____

_____

_____

I AM TAKING CARE OF MYSELF TODAY BY...

_____

_____

_____

TODAY I AM LOOKING FORWARD TO...

_____

_____

_____

SOMETHING GOOD THAT HAPPENED TODAY...

_____

_____

_____

I will get through this.

TODAY I AM FEELING...

_____

_____

_____

I AM TAKING CARE OF MYSELF TODAY BY...

_____

_____

_____

TODAY I AM LOOKING FORWARD TO...

_____

_____

_____

SOMETHING GOOD THAT HAPPENED TODAY...

_____

_____

_____

My home is filled with laughter.

TODAY I AM FEELING...

_____

_____

_____

I AM TAKING CARE OF MYSELF TODAY BY...

_____

_____

_____

TODAY I AM LOOKING FORWARD TO...

_____

_____

_____

SOMETHING GOOD THAT HAPPENED TODAY...

_____

_____

_____

I focus on the good in life.

TODAY I AM FEELING...

_____

_____

_____

I AM TAKING CARE OF MYSELF TODAY BY...

_____

_____

_____

TODAY I AM LOOKING FORWARD TO...

_____

_____

_____

SOMETHING GOOD THAT HAPPENED TODAY...

_____

_____

_____

I make sound decisions.

TODAY I AM FEELING...

_____

_____

_____

I AM TAKING CARE OF MYSELF TODAY BY...

_____

_____

_____

TODAY I AM LOOKING FORWARD TO...

_____

_____

_____

SOMETHING GOOD THAT HAPPENED TODAY...

_____

_____

_____

I got this.

TODAY I AM FEELING...

_____

_____

_____

I AM TAKING CARE OF MYSELF TODAY BY...

_____

_____

_____

TODAY I AM LOOKING FORWARD TO...

_____

_____

_____

SOMETHING GOOD THAT HAPPENED TODAY...

_____

_____

_____

I love my body.

TODAY I AM FEELING...

_____

_____

_____

I AM TAKING CARE OF MYSELF TODAY BY...

_____

_____

_____

TODAY I AM LOOKING FORWARD TO...

_____

_____

_____

SOMETHING GOOD THAT HAPPENED TODAY...

_____

_____

_____

I cheer myself on.

TODAY I AM FEELING...

_____

_____

_____

I AM TAKING CARE OF MYSELF TODAY BY...

_____

_____

_____

TODAY I AM LOOKING FORWARD TO...

_____

_____

_____

SOMETHING GOOD THAT HAPPENED TODAY...

_____

_____

_____

I am confident.

TODAY I AM FEELING...

_____

_____

_____

I AM TAKING CARE OF MYSELF TODAY BY...

_____

_____

_____

TODAY I AM LOOKING FORWARD TO...

_____

_____

_____

SOMETHING GOOD THAT HAPPENED TODAY...

_____

_____

_____

I view each experience through eyes of love.

TODAY I AM FEELING...

_____

_____

_____

I AM TAKING CARE OF MYSELF TODAY BY...

_____

_____

_____

TODAY I AM LOOKING FORWARD TO...

_____

_____

_____

SOMETHING GOOD THAT HAPPENED TODAY...

_____

_____

_____

I show up for myself.

TODAY I AM FEELING...

_____

_____

_____

I AM TAKING CARE OF MYSELF TODAY BY...

_____

_____

_____

TODAY I AM LOOKING FORWARD TO...

_____

_____

_____

SOMETHING GOOD THAT HAPPENED TODAY...

_____

_____

_____

Mistakes are only lessons.

TODAY I AM FEELING...

_____

_____

_____

I AM TAKING CARE OF MYSELF TODAY BY...

_____

_____

_____

TODAY I AM LOOKING FORWARD TO...

_____

_____

_____

SOMETHING GOOD THAT HAPPENED TODAY...

_____

_____

_____

I get plenty of rest.

TODAY I AM FEELING...

_____

_____

_____

I AM TAKING CARE OF MYSELF TODAY BY...

_____

_____

_____

TODAY I AM LOOKING FORWARD TO...

_____

_____

_____

SOMETHING GOOD THAT HAPPENED TODAY...

_____

_____

_____

I allow myself to dream.

TODAY I AM FEELING...

_____

_____

_____

I AM TAKING CARE OF MYSELF TODAY BY...

_____

_____

_____

TODAY I AM LOOKING FORWARD TO...

_____

_____

_____

SOMETHING GOOD THAT HAPPENED TODAY...

_____

_____

_____

I am always greeted with kindness.

TODAY I AM FEELING...

_____

_____

_____

I AM TAKING CARE OF MYSELF TODAY BY...

_____

_____

_____

TODAY I AM LOOKING FORWARD TO...

_____

_____

_____

SOMETHING GOOD THAT HAPPENED TODAY...

_____

_____

_____

I take loving care of my body.

TODAY I AM FEELING...

_____

_____

_____

I AM TAKING CARE OF MYSELF TODAY BY...

_____

_____

_____

TODAY I AM LOOKING FORWARD TO...

_____

_____

_____

SOMETHING GOOD THAT HAPPENED TODAY...

_____

_____

_____

I appreciate myself.

TODAY I AM FEELING...

_____

_____

_____

I AM TAKING CARE OF MYSELF TODAY BY...

_____

_____

_____

TODAY I AM LOOKING FORWARD TO...

_____

_____

_____

SOMETHING GOOD THAT HAPPENED TODAY...

_____

_____

_____

My feelings are valid.

TODAY I AM FEELING...

_____

_____

_____

I AM TAKING CARE OF MYSELF TODAY BY...

_____

_____

_____

TODAY I AM LOOKING FORWARD TO...

_____

_____

_____

SOMETHING GOOD THAT HAPPENED TODAY...

_____

_____

_____

I find joy in this moment.

TODAY I AM FEELING...

_____

_____

_____

I AM TAKING CARE OF MYSELF TODAY BY...

_____

_____

_____

TODAY I AM LOOKING FORWARD TO...

_____

_____

_____

SOMETHING GOOD THAT HAPPENED TODAY...

_____

_____

_____

I love myself.

TODAY I AM FEELING...

_____

_____

_____

I AM TAKING CARE OF MYSELF TODAY BY...

_____

_____

_____

TODAY I AM LOOKING FORWARD TO...

_____

_____

_____

SOMETHING GOOD THAT HAPPENED TODAY...

_____

_____

_____

I am thankful for my life.

TODAY I AM FEELING...

_____

_____

_____

I AM TAKING CARE OF MYSELF TODAY BY...

_____

_____

_____

TODAY I AM LOOKING FORWARD TO...

_____

_____

_____

SOMETHING GOOD THAT HAPPENED TODAY...

_____

_____

_____

I embrace change.

TODAY I AM FEELING...

_____

_____

_____

I AM TAKING CARE OF MYSELF TODAY BY...

_____

_____

_____

TODAY I AM LOOKING FORWARD TO...

_____

_____

_____

SOMETHING GOOD THAT HAPPENED TODAY...

_____

_____

_____

I honor myself.

TODAY I AM FEELING...

_____

_____

_____

I AM TAKING CARE OF MYSELF TODAY BY...

_____

_____

_____

TODAY I AM LOOKING FORWARD TO...

_____

_____

_____

SOMETHING GOOD THAT HAPPENED TODAY...

_____

_____

_____

I am free from worry.

TODAY I AM FEELING...

_____

_____

_____

I AM TAKING CARE OF MYSELF TODAY BY...

_____

_____

_____

TODAY I AM LOOKING FORWARD TO...

_____

_____

_____

SOMETHING GOOD THAT HAPPENED TODAY...

_____

_____

_____

My home is filled with love.

TODAY I AM FEELING...

_____

_____

_____

I AM TAKING CARE OF MYSELF TODAY BY...

_____

_____

_____

TODAY I AM LOOKING FORWARD TO...

_____

_____

_____

SOMETHING GOOD THAT HAPPENED TODAY...

_____

_____

_____

I allow myself to heal.

TODAY I AM FEELING...

_____

_____

_____

I AM TAKING CARE OF MYSELF TODAY BY...

_____

_____

_____

TODAY I AM LOOKING FORWARD TO...

_____

_____

_____

SOMETHING GOOD THAT HAPPENED TODAY...

_____

_____

_____

I take deep breaths.

TODAY I AM FEELING...

_____

_____

_____

I AM TAKING CARE OF MYSELF TODAY BY...

_____

_____

_____

TODAY I AM LOOKING FORWARD TO...

_____

_____

_____

SOMETHING GOOD THAT HAPPENED TODAY...

_____

_____

_____

I forgive myself.

TODAY I AM FEELING...

_____

_____

_____

I AM TAKING CARE OF MYSELF TODAY BY...

_____

_____

_____

TODAY I AM LOOKING FORWARD TO...

_____

_____

_____

SOMETHING GOOD THAT HAPPENED TODAY...

_____

_____

_____

I am a good person.

TODAY I AM FEELING...

_____

_____

_____

I AM TAKING CARE OF MYSELF TODAY BY...

_____

_____

_____

TODAY I AM LOOKING FORWARD TO...

_____

_____

_____

SOMETHING GOOD THAT HAPPENED TODAY...

_____

_____

_____

Wellness surrounds me.

TODAY I AM FEELING...

_____
_____
_____

I AM TAKING CARE OF MYSELF TODAY BY...

_____
_____
_____

TODAY I AM LOOKING FORWARD TO...

_____
_____
_____

SOMETHING GOOD THAT HAPPENED TODAY...

_____
_____
_____

I think positive thoughts.

TODAY I AM FEELING...

_____

_____

_____

I AM TAKING CARE OF MYSELF TODAY BY...

_____

_____

_____

TODAY I AM LOOKING FORWARD TO...

_____

_____

_____

SOMETHING GOOD THAT HAPPENED TODAY...

_____

_____

_____

Things always work out.

TODAY I AM FEELING...

_____

_____

_____

I AM TAKING CARE OF MYSELF TODAY BY...

_____

_____

_____

TODAY I AM LOOKING FORWARD TO...

_____

_____

_____

SOMETHING GOOD THAT HAPPENED TODAY...

_____

_____

_____

I eat healthy foods.

TODAY I AM FEELING...

_____

_____

_____

I AM TAKING CARE OF MYSELF TODAY BY...

_____

_____

_____

TODAY I AM LOOKING FORWARD TO...

_____

_____

_____

SOMETHING GOOD THAT HAPPENED TODAY...

_____

_____

_____

I am filled with joy.

TODAY I AM FEELING...

_____

_____

_____

I AM TAKING CARE OF MYSELF TODAY BY...

_____

_____

_____

TODAY I AM LOOKING FORWARD TO...

_____

_____

_____

SOMETHING GOOD THAT HAPPENED TODAY...

_____

_____

_____

I deserve a peaceful life.

TODAY I AM FEELING...

_____

_____

_____

I AM TAKING CARE OF MYSELF TODAY BY...

_____

_____

_____

TODAY I AM LOOKING FORWARD TO...

_____

_____

_____

SOMETHING GOOD THAT HAPPENED TODAY...

_____

_____

_____

I find happiness within.

TODAY I AM FEELING...

_____

_____

_____

I AM TAKING CARE OF MYSELF TODAY BY...

_____

_____

_____

TODAY I AM LOOKING FORWARD TO...

_____

_____

_____

SOMETHING GOOD THAT HAPPENED TODAY...

_____

_____

_____

All is well.

TODAY I AM FEELING...

_____

_____

_____

I AM TAKING CARE OF MYSELF TODAY BY...

_____

_____

_____

TODAY I AM LOOKING FORWARD TO...

_____

_____

_____

SOMETHING GOOD THAT HAPPENED TODAY...

_____

_____

_____

I believe in myself.

TODAY I AM FEELING...

_____

_____

_____

I AM TAKING CARE OF MYSELF TODAY BY...

_____

_____

_____

TODAY I AM LOOKING FORWARD TO...

_____

_____

_____

SOMETHING GOOD THAT HAPPENED TODAY...

_____

_____

_____

Exercise helps me clear my mind.

TODAY I AM FEELING...

_____

_____

_____

I AM TAKING CARE OF MYSELF TODAY BY...

_____

_____

_____

TODAY I AM LOOKING FORWARD TO...

_____

_____

_____

SOMETHING GOOD THAT HAPPENED TODAY...

_____

_____

_____

I drink lots of water.

TODAY I AM FEELING...

_____

_____

_____

I AM TAKING CARE OF MYSELF TODAY BY...

_____

_____

_____

TODAY I AM LOOKING FORWARD TO...

_____

_____

_____

SOMETHING GOOD THAT HAPPENED TODAY...

_____

_____

_____

I make time for myself each day.

TODAY I AM FEELING...

_____
_____
_____

I AM TAKING CARE OF MYSELF TODAY BY...

_____
_____
_____

TODAY I AM LOOKING FORWARD TO...

_____
_____
_____

SOMETHING GOOD THAT HAPPENED TODAY...

_____
_____
_____

I do not have to explain myself.

TODAY I AM FEELING...

_____

_____

_____

I AM TAKING CARE OF MYSELF TODAY BY...

_____

_____

_____

TODAY I AM LOOKING FORWARD TO...

_____

_____

_____

SOMETHING GOOD THAT HAPPENED TODAY...

_____

_____

_____

Beauty surrounds me.

TODAY I AM FEELING...

_____

_____

_____

I AM TAKING CARE OF MYSELF TODAY BY...

_____

_____

_____

TODAY I AM LOOKING FORWARD TO...

_____

_____

_____

SOMETHING GOOD THAT HAPPENED TODAY...

_____

_____

_____

I deserve to be happy.

TODAY I AM FEELING...

_____

_____

_____

I AM TAKING CARE OF MYSELF TODAY BY...

_____

_____

_____

TODAY I AM LOOKING FORWARD TO...

_____

_____

_____

SOMETHING GOOD THAT HAPPENED TODAY...

_____

_____

_____

I have a peaceful home.

TODAY I AM FEELING...

_____

_____

_____

I AM TAKING CARE OF MYSELF TODAY BY...

_____

_____

_____

TODAY I AM LOOKING FORWARD TO...

_____

_____

_____

SOMETHING GOOD THAT HAPPENED TODAY...

_____

_____

_____

I am seen and heard.

TODAY I AM FEELING...

_____

_____

_____

I AM TAKING CARE OF MYSELF TODAY BY...

_____

_____

_____

TODAY I AM LOOKING FORWARD TO...

_____

_____

_____

SOMETHING GOOD THAT HAPPENED TODAY...

_____

_____

_____

I stand up for myself.

TODAY I AM FEELING...

_____

_____

_____

I AM TAKING CARE OF MYSELF TODAY BY...

_____

_____

_____

TODAY I AM LOOKING FORWARD TO...

_____

_____

_____

SOMETHING GOOD THAT HAPPENED TODAY...

_____

_____

_____

I am valued.

TODAY I AM FEELING...

_____

_____

_____

I AM TAKING CARE OF MYSELF TODAY BY...

_____

_____

_____

TODAY I AM LOOKING FORWARD TO...

_____

_____

_____

SOMETHING GOOD THAT HAPPENED TODAY...

_____

_____

_____

I am worthy.

TODAY I AM FEELING...

_____

_____

_____

I AM TAKING CARE OF MYSELF TODAY BY...

_____

_____

_____

TODAY I AM LOOKING FORWARD TO...

_____

_____

_____

SOMETHING GOOD THAT HAPPENED TODAY...

_____

_____

_____

71

I am enough.

TODAY I AM FEELING...

_____

_____

_____

I AM TAKING CARE OF MYSELF TODAY BY...

_____

_____

_____

TODAY I AM LOOKING FORWARD TO...

_____

_____

_____

SOMETHING GOOD THAT HAPPENED TODAY...

_____

_____

_____

I give myself permission to be happy.

TODAY I AM FEELING...

_____

_____

_____

I AM TAKING CARE OF MYSELF TODAY BY...

_____

_____

_____

TODAY I AM LOOKING FORWARD TO...

_____

_____

_____

SOMETHING GOOD THAT HAPPENED TODAY...

_____

_____

_____

I am surrounded by peace.

TODAY I AM FEELING...

_____

_____

_____

I AM TAKING CARE OF MYSELF TODAY BY...

_____

_____

_____

TODAY I AM LOOKING FORWARD TO...

_____

_____

_____

SOMETHING GOOD THAT HAPPENED TODAY...

_____

_____

_____

I am always at the right place at the right time.

TODAY I AM FEELING...

_____

_____

_____

I AM TAKING CARE OF MYSELF TODAY BY...

_____

_____

_____

TODAY I AM LOOKING FORWARD TO...

_____

_____

_____

SOMETHING GOOD THAT HAPPENED TODAY...

_____

_____

_____

Joy fills my home.

TODAY I AM FEELING...

_____

_____

_____

I AM TAKING CARE OF MYSELF TODAY BY...

_____

_____

_____

TODAY I AM LOOKING FORWARD TO...

_____

_____

_____

SOMETHING GOOD THAT HAPPENED TODAY...

_____

_____

_____

I compliment myself.

TODAY I AM FEELING...

_____

_____

_____

I AM TAKING CARE OF MYSELF TODAY BY...

_____

_____

_____

TODAY I AM LOOKING FORWARD TO...

_____

_____

_____

SOMETHING GOOD THAT HAPPENED TODAY...

_____

_____

_____

I only speak what I want to see in my world.

TODAY I AM FEELING...

_____

_____

_____

I AM TAKING CARE OF MYSELF TODAY BY...

_____

_____

_____

TODAY I AM LOOKING FORWARD TO...

_____

_____

_____

SOMETHING GOOD THAT HAPPENED TODAY...

_____

_____

_____

I make time for fun.

TODAY I AM FEELING...

_____

_____

_____

I AM TAKING CARE OF MYSELF TODAY BY...

_____

_____

_____

TODAY I AM LOOKING FORWARD TO...

_____

_____

_____

SOMETHING GOOD THAT HAPPENED TODAY...

_____

_____

_____

Today, I choose me.

TODAY I AM FEELING...

_____

_____

_____

I AM TAKING CARE OF MYSELF TODAY BY...

_____

_____

_____

TODAY I AM LOOKING FORWARD TO...

_____

_____

_____

SOMETHING GOOD THAT HAPPENED TODAY...

_____

_____

_____

All of my needs are met in abundance.

TODAY I AM FEELING...

_____
_____
_____

I AM TAKING CARE OF MYSELF TODAY BY...

_____
_____
_____

TODAY I AM LOOKING FORWARD TO...

_____
_____
_____

SOMETHING GOOD THAT HAPPENED TODAY...

_____
_____
_____

My mind is at ease.

TODAY I AM FEELING...

_____

_____

_____

I AM TAKING CARE OF MYSELF TODAY BY...

_____

_____

_____

TODAY I AM LOOKING FORWARD TO...

_____

_____

_____

SOMETHING GOOD THAT HAPPENED TODAY...

_____

_____

_____

I lovingly release the past.

TODAY I AM FEELING...

_____

_____

_____

I AM TAKING CARE OF MYSELF TODAY BY...

_____

_____

_____

TODAY I AM LOOKING FORWARD TO...

_____

_____

_____

SOMETHING GOOD THAT HAPPENED TODAY...

_____

_____

_____

My happiness is non-negotiable.

TODAY I AM FEELING...

_____

_____

_____

I AM TAKING CARE OF MYSELF TODAY BY...

_____

_____

_____

TODAY I AM LOOKING FORWARD TO...

_____

_____

_____

SOMETHING GOOD THAT HAPPENED TODAY...

_____

_____

_____

I give thanks for all that is good in my life.

TODAY I AM FEELING...

_____

_____

_____

I AM TAKING CARE OF MYSELF TODAY BY...

_____

_____

_____

TODAY I AM LOOKING FORWARD TO...

_____

_____

_____

SOMETHING GOOD THAT HAPPENED TODAY...

_____

_____

_____

I choose to be at peace.

TODAY I AM FEELING...

_____

_____

_____

I AM TAKING CARE OF MYSELF TODAY BY...

_____

_____

_____

TODAY I AM LOOKING FORWARD TO...

_____

_____

_____

SOMETHING GOOD THAT HAPPENED TODAY...

_____

_____

_____

I radiate love.

TODAY I AM FEELING...

_____

_____

_____

I AM TAKING CARE OF MYSELF TODAY BY...

_____

_____

_____

TODAY I AM LOOKING FORWARD TO...

_____

_____

_____

SOMETHING GOOD THAT HAPPENED TODAY...

_____

_____

_____

I deserve to rest.

TODAY I AM FEELING...

_____

_____

_____

I AM TAKING CARE OF MYSELF TODAY BY...

_____

_____

_____

TODAY I AM LOOKING FORWARD TO...

_____

_____

_____

SOMETHING GOOD THAT HAPPENED TODAY...

_____

_____

_____

There is a solution for every problem.

TODAY I AM FEELING...

_____

_____

_____

I AM TAKING CARE OF MYSELF TODAY BY...

_____

_____

_____

TODAY I AM LOOKING FORWARD TO...

_____

_____

_____

SOMETHING GOOD THAT HAPPENED TODAY...

_____

_____

_____

I reclaim my power.

TODAY I AM FEELING...

_____

_____

_____

I AM TAKING CARE OF MYSELF TODAY BY...

_____

_____

_____

TODAY I AM LOOKING FORWARD TO...

_____

_____

_____

SOMETHING GOOD THAT HAPPENED TODAY...

_____

_____

_____

I define success for myself.

TODAY I AM FEELING...

_____

_____

_____

I AM TAKING CARE OF MYSELF TODAY BY...

_____

_____

_____

TODAY I AM LOOKING FORWARD TO...

_____

_____

_____

SOMETHING GOOD THAT HAPPENED TODAY...

_____

_____

_____

Peace fills my life.

TODAY I AM FEELING...

_____

_____

_____

I AM TAKING CARE OF MYSELF TODAY BY...

_____

_____

_____

TODAY I AM LOOKING FORWARD TO...

_____

_____

_____

SOMETHING GOOD THAT HAPPENED TODAY...

_____

_____

_____

I am nurtured and cared for.

TODAY I AM FEELING...

_____

_____

_____

I AM TAKING CARE OF MYSELF TODAY BY...

_____

_____

_____

TODAY I AM LOOKING FORWARD TO...

_____

_____

_____

SOMETHING GOOD THAT HAPPENED TODAY...

_____

_____

_____

I set healthy boundaries.

TODAY I AM FEELING...

_____

_____

_____

I AM TAKING CARE OF MYSELF TODAY BY...

_____

_____

_____

TODAY I AM LOOKING FORWARD TO...

_____

_____

_____

SOMETHING GOOD THAT HAPPENED TODAY...

_____

_____

_____

My home is clean and organized.

TODAY I AM FEELING...

_____

_____

_____

I AM TAKING CARE OF MYSELF TODAY BY...

_____

_____

_____

TODAY I AM LOOKING FORWARD TO...

_____

_____

_____

SOMETHING GOOD THAT HAPPENED TODAY...

_____

_____

_____

I speak kindly of myself and others.

TODAY I AM FEELING...

_____

_____

_____

I AM TAKING CARE OF MYSELF TODAY BY...

_____

_____

_____

TODAY I AM LOOKING FORWARD TO...

_____

_____

_____

SOMETHING GOOD THAT HAPPENED TODAY...

_____

_____

_____

I recognize my own needs.

TODAY I AM FEELING...

_____

_____

_____

I AM TAKING CARE OF MYSELF TODAY BY...

_____

_____

_____

TODAY I AM LOOKING FORWARD TO...

_____

_____

_____

SOMETHING GOOD THAT HAPPENED TODAY...

_____

_____

_____

I ask for help when I need it.

TODAY I AM FEELING...

_____

_____

_____

I AM TAKING CARE OF MYSELF TODAY BY...

_____

_____

_____

TODAY I AM LOOKING FORWARD TO...

_____

_____

_____

SOMETHING GOOD THAT HAPPENED TODAY...

_____

_____

_____

I am capable.

TODAY I AM FEELING...

_____

_____

_____

I AM TAKING CARE OF MYSELF TODAY BY...

_____

_____

_____

TODAY I AM LOOKING FORWARD TO...

_____

_____

_____

SOMETHING GOOD THAT HAPPENED TODAY...

_____

_____

_____

I make time to celebrate.

TODAY I AM FEELING...

_____

_____

_____

I AM TAKING CARE OF MYSELF TODAY BY...

_____

_____

_____

TODAY I AM LOOKING FORWARD TO...

_____

_____

_____

SOMETHING GOOD THAT HAPPENED TODAY...

_____

_____

_____

I dream big.

TODAY I AM FEELING...

_____

_____

_____

I AM TAKING CARE OF MYSELF TODAY BY...

_____

_____

_____

TODAY I AM LOOKING FORWARD TO...

_____

_____

_____

SOMETHING GOOD THAT HAPPENED TODAY...

_____

_____

_____

I am patient with myself.

TODAY I AM FEELING...

_____

_____

_____

I AM TAKING CARE OF MYSELF TODAY BY...

_____

_____

_____

TODAY I AM LOOKING FORWARD TO...

_____

_____

_____

SOMETHING GOOD THAT HAPPENED TODAY...

_____

_____

_____

I honor my feelings.

TODAY I AM FEELING...

_____

_____

_____

I AM TAKING CARE OF MYSELF TODAY BY...

_____

_____

_____

TODAY I AM LOOKING FORWARD TO...

_____

_____

_____

SOMETHING GOOD THAT HAPPENED TODAY...

_____

_____

_____

My home is filled with joy.

TODAY I AM FEELING...

_____

_____

_____

I AM TAKING CARE OF MYSELF TODAY BY...

_____

_____

_____

TODAY I AM LOOKING FORWARD TO...

_____

_____

_____

SOMETHING GOOD THAT HAPPENED TODAY...

_____

_____

_____

The love I give out comes back to me.

TODAY I AM FEELING...

_____

_____

_____

I AM TAKING CARE OF MYSELF TODAY BY...

_____

_____

_____

TODAY I AM LOOKING FORWARD TO...

_____

_____

_____

SOMETHING GOOD THAT HAPPENED TODAY...

_____

_____

_____

It is easy for me to say no.

TODAY I AM FEELING...

_____

_____

_____

I AM TAKING CARE OF MYSELF TODAY BY...

_____

_____

_____

TODAY I AM LOOKING FORWARD TO...

_____

_____

_____

SOMETHING GOOD THAT HAPPENED TODAY...

_____

_____

_____

I cherish this day.

TODAY I AM FEELING...

_____

_____

_____

I AM TAKING CARE OF MYSELF TODAY BY...

_____

_____

_____

TODAY I AM LOOKING FORWARD TO...

_____

_____

_____

SOMETHING GOOD THAT HAPPENED TODAY...

_____

_____

_____

I handle challenges with ease.

TODAY I AM FEELING...

_____

_____

_____

I AM TAKING CARE OF MYSELF TODAY BY...

_____

_____

_____

TODAY I AM LOOKING FORWARD TO...

_____

_____

_____

SOMETHING GOOD THAT HAPPENED TODAY...

_____

_____

_____

I have everything I need.

TODAY I AM FEELING...

_____

_____

_____

I AM TAKING CARE OF MYSELF TODAY BY...

_____

_____

_____

TODAY I AM LOOKING FORWARD TO...

_____

_____

_____

SOMETHING GOOD THAT HAPPENED TODAY...

_____

_____

_____

I choose joy.

TODAY I AM FEELING...

_____

_____

_____

I AM TAKING CARE OF MYSELF TODAY BY...

_____

_____

_____

TODAY I AM LOOKING FORWARD TO...

_____

_____

_____

SOMETHING GOOD THAT HAPPENED TODAY...

_____

_____

_____

I speak up for myself.

TODAY I AM FEELING...

_____

_____

_____

I AM TAKING CARE OF MYSELF TODAY BY...

_____

_____

_____

TODAY I AM LOOKING FORWARD TO...

_____

_____

_____

SOMETHING GOOD THAT HAPPENED TODAY...

_____

_____

_____

I am blessed.

TODAY I AM FEELING...

_____

_____

_____

I AM TAKING CARE OF MYSELF TODAY BY...

_____

_____

_____

TODAY I AM LOOKING FORWARD TO...

_____

_____

_____

SOMETHING GOOD THAT HAPPENED TODAY...

_____

_____

_____

I am worthy of harmony.

TODAY I AM FEELING...

_____

_____

_____

I AM TAKING CARE OF MYSELF TODAY BY...

_____

_____

_____

TODAY I AM LOOKING FORWARD TO...

_____

_____

_____

SOMETHING GOOD THAT HAPPENED TODAY...

_____

_____

_____

I am deeply fulfilled.

TODAY I AM FEELING...

_____

_____

_____

I AM TAKING CARE OF MYSELF TODAY BY...

_____

_____

_____

TODAY I AM LOOKING FORWARD TO...

_____

_____

_____

SOMETHING GOOD THAT HAPPENED TODAY...

_____

_____

_____

I am satisfied with life.

TODAY I AM FEELING...

_____

_____

_____

I AM TAKING CARE OF MYSELF TODAY BY...

_____

_____

_____

TODAY I AM LOOKING FORWARD TO...

_____

_____

_____

SOMETHING GOOD THAT HAPPENED TODAY...

_____

_____

_____

All of my prayers are answered.

TODAY I AM FEELING...

_____

_____

_____

I AM TAKING CARE OF MYSELF TODAY BY...

_____

_____

_____

TODAY I AM LOOKING FORWARD TO...

_____

_____

_____

SOMETHING GOOD THAT HAPPENED TODAY...

_____

_____

_____

I can always find something to be grateful for.

TODAY I AM FEELING...

_____

_____

_____

I AM TAKING CARE OF MYSELF TODAY BY...

_____

_____

_____

TODAY I AM LOOKING FORWARD TO...

_____

_____

_____

SOMETHING GOOD THAT HAPPENED TODAY...

_____

_____

_____

I expect good things to happen.

TODAY I AM FEELING...

_____

_____

_____

I AM TAKING CARE OF MYSELF TODAY BY...

_____

_____

_____

TODAY I AM LOOKING FORWARD TO...

_____

_____

_____

SOMETHING GOOD THAT HAPPENED TODAY...

_____

_____

_____

I am calm.

TODAY I AM FEELING...

_____

_____

_____

I AM TAKING CARE OF MYSELF TODAY BY...

_____

_____

_____

TODAY I AM LOOKING FORWARD TO...

_____

_____

_____

SOMETHING GOOD THAT HAPPENED TODAY...

_____

_____

_____

I live a joyous and harmonious life.

TODAY I AM FEELING...

_____

_____

_____

I AM TAKING CARE OF MYSELF TODAY BY...

_____

_____

_____

TODAY I AM LOOKING FORWARD TO...

_____

_____

_____

SOMETHING GOOD THAT HAPPENED TODAY...

_____

_____

_____

I do not overextend myself.

TODAY I AM FEELING...

_____

_____

_____

I AM TAKING CARE OF MYSELF TODAY BY...

_____

_____

_____

TODAY I AM LOOKING FORWARD TO...

_____

_____

_____

SOMETHING GOOD THAT HAPPENED TODAY...

_____

_____

_____

I am worthy of my own time.

TODAY I AM FEELING...

_____

_____

_____

I AM TAKING CARE OF MYSELF TODAY BY...

_____

_____

_____

TODAY I AM LOOKING FORWARD TO...

_____

_____

_____

SOMETHING GOOD THAT HAPPENED TODAY...

_____

_____

_____

I welcome abundance.

TODAY I AM FEELING...

_____

_____

_____

I AM TAKING CARE OF MYSELF TODAY BY...

_____

_____

_____

TODAY I AM LOOKING FORWARD TO...

_____

_____

_____

SOMETHING GOOD THAT HAPPENED TODAY...

_____

_____

_____

I am willing to make positive changes.

TODAY I AM FEELING...

_____

_____

_____

I AM TAKING CARE OF MYSELF TODAY BY...

_____

_____

_____

TODAY I AM LOOKING FORWARD TO...

_____

_____

_____

SOMETHING GOOD THAT HAPPENED TODAY...

_____

_____

_____

I buy nice things for myself.

TODAY I AM FEELING...

_____

_____

_____

I AM TAKING CARE OF MYSELF TODAY BY...

_____

_____

_____

TODAY I AM LOOKING FORWARD TO...

_____

_____

_____

SOMETHING GOOD THAT HAPPENED TODAY...

_____

_____

_____

I make time to connect with friends and loved ones.

TODAY I AM FEELING...

_____

_____

_____

I AM TAKING CARE OF MYSELF TODAY BY...

_____

_____

_____

TODAY I AM LOOKING FORWARD TO...

_____

_____

_____

SOMETHING GOOD THAT HAPPENED TODAY...

_____

_____

_____

I am at ease in my home.

TODAY I AM FEELING...

_____

_____

_____

I AM TAKING CARE OF MYSELF TODAY BY...

_____

_____

_____

TODAY I AM LOOKING FORWARD TO...

_____

_____

_____

SOMETHING GOOD THAT HAPPENED TODAY...

_____

_____

_____

Made in the USA
Middletown, DE
25 March 2023

27645257R00076